ROBERT BURTON

ANIMAL HOMES

DESERTS

photographs by Oxford Scientific Films

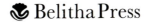
Belitha Press

First published in Great Britain in 1991 by
Belitha Press Limited
31 Newington Green, London N16 9PU
Printed in Singapore for Imago Publishing

ISBN 1 85561 043 4

British Library Cataloguing in Publication Data
CIP data for this book is available from the British Library

The publishers wish to thank the following for permission
to reproduce copyright material:

Oxford Scientific Films and individual copyright
holders on the following pages: Anthony Bannister 5, 17,
Eyal Bartov 18, 20, Malcolm Coe 4, J. A. L. Cooke 8, 16,
David Curl back cover, Animals Animals/E. R.
Degginger 19, Jack Dermid 11, Michael Fogden 7, 13,
Mantis Wildlife Films/Jim Frazier 12, 14, Animals
Animals/John Gerbach 22, Mickey Gibson 2, 3, R. J. B.
Goodale 9, C. W. Helliwell title page, Rodger Jackman
6, 15, Zigmund Leszczynski front cover, 10, 21, Stan
Osolinski 23

Deserts are very dry places. Less than 25 centimetres of rain falls in a year. This is about a quarter of the rainfall in Northern Europe. Some deserts do not get any rain from one year to the next. Deserts are also very hot.

Desert people use camels for making long journeys. Camels can live a long time without eating or drinking. They can get enough water from juicy plants so that they do not have to drink for several days. If they cannot get water from plants camels slowly dry up. When they reach an **oasis** or a well, they will drink an enormous amount. A camel can drink 130 litres of water in a few minutes.

Baby camels are born without humps. They can walk and follow their mothers when they are only one day old. A baby camel will stay with its mother for up to four years.

All animals that live in the desert must have some way of getting water. They must also avoid getting too hot. Gemsboks are a kind of antelope. They live in the Kalahari Desert of southern Africa. They get their water by eating juicy cucumbers and melons. Gemsboks try to keep cool by standing in the shade of a tree.

Gerbils are often kept as pets. There are many different kinds of gerbil living in dry countries of Africa and Asia. This is a Mongolian gerbil. Their yellowish fur helps to **camouflage** the gerbils against the sand of the desert. This means that **predators** cannot find them and eat them.

Gerbils dig burrows to hide from the sun during the day. Gerbils help to keep the air in their burrows cool by blocking the entrance with sand. This stops hot air from getting in.

White-sided jack rabbits live in the deserts of the south-west United States and northern Mexico. They try to sit in the shade to keep out of the sun. When there are no bushes for shelter, the white-sided jack rabbit's long ears act like radiators. They help it to get rid of its body heat and keep cool.

White-sided jack rabbits eat cactus plants. They nibble very carefully around the cactus spines to make a hole in the plant. They can then eat the soft flesh inside without getting pricked by the sharp spines.

The jerboa looks like a tiny kangaroo but it is actually a kind of mouse. It is only about 12 centimetres long but it can hop 3 metres at a time.

Jerboas live in the driest deserts of Africa and Asia. When it is very hot they stay in their burrows and go to sleep until it gets cooler. The jerboas store food in their burrows. This means that they have something to eat when it is too hot to go out. Their babies are born in the burrows.

The rabbit-eared bandicoot of Australia has large ears too. It is also known as the great bilby. It is a **marsupial**, like the kangaroo and koala. Bandicoot babies are tiny when they are born. They live in their mother's pouch, like baby kangaroos do, until they are about seven weeks old. Then they are able to run about.

Gopher tortoises live in the southern United States. They have front feet shaped like spades. They use these for digging in soft sandy soil. They are used to make burrows up to 11 metres long.

Gopher tortoises lay their eggs in a pit that they dig in the soil. The eggs are kept warm by the hot soil. When the eggs hatch, the baby tortoises dig themselves out of the soil and crawl away. They never see their parents.

This gopher tortoise is crawling back to its burrow in the morning before the sun gets hot and bakes it. Like all tortoises it is very slow and can only crawl at 0.5 kilometres per hour. This is about ten times slower than a person walks.

The thorny devils of Australia look dangerous but they are harmless. The spikes that cover their bodies protect them from **predators** that might try to eat them. Thorny devils only eat ants. One thorny devil might eat several thousand ants in one meal.

Thorny devils have an unusual way of getting water. If a drop of water falls on a thorny devil's back, the water spreads out. It runs along tiny grooves in the skin and quickly reaches the mouth of the lizard where it is swallowed.

The gila (pronounced 'heela') monster is one of only two kinds of poisonous lizards. The other is a close relative of the gila monster called the beaded lizard. Like snakes, these lizards inject poison when they bite their **prey**. The poison is not very strong and rarely kills healthy adult humans.

Amphibians, such as frogs and toads, are water-loving animals. Their skins are not properly waterproof and their bodies will quickly dry up if they are not kept moist. They also need pools in which to lay their **spawn**.

A few amphibians can survive in deserts. Usually they live near rivers or pools. They dig deep into the ground where it is cooler and damper. The water-holding frogs of Australia store water in their bodies so that they do not dry up.

Desert amphibians sometimes have to stay underground for years until it rains. When it does rain, they come out of their holes to lay their spawn in pools and puddles. The tadpoles that hatch from the spawn grow up very quickly and turn into adult frogs or toads before the water disappears. The eggs of the spadefoot toads of America hatch only one day after they are laid. Just three weeks later the tadpoles turn into toads. Ordinary toads take several months to grow up.

This beetle is digging itself into the sand. It has spent the night walking and looking for food. When the sun rises, the beetle must hide from the heat. It also has to hide because all sorts of animals, such as birds, foxes and lizards, will try to catch and eat it.

Geckos are a kind of **reptile**. Desert geckos have webbed feet. These help them to walk on very soft sand. This gecko is eating a cricket. The cricket's blood will provide the gecko with water so that it does not have to drink.

Fennecs are small foxes that live in the Sahara Desert. The head and body of a fennec measure only 40-45 centimetres but its huge ears are 15 centimetres long. Their ears give fennecs very good hearing. They also act like radiators to help them keep cool, just like the ears of the white-sided jack rabbits.

Fennecs dig their burrows in spring so that there is a cool moist den for their cubs. When the cubs are old enough to eat solid food their father brings them insects, snakes, gerbils and other small animals to eat.

Pumas, also known as cougars or mountain lions, live in America. They live in forests, up mountains and on prairies. They are also found in deserts. Pumas often live on the edge of deserts. Sometimes they go into the driest parts in search of **prey**. A puma can get enough to drink from the blood of the animals it catches.

20

Several kinds of poisonous snakes live in deserts. This is a sand viper from the Sahara Desert. It is burying itself in the sand so that only its head will show. This makes it difficult for the animals it catches as prey to see it.

Snakes find it difficult to crawl in deserts because their bodies slip in the soft sand. Instead they move by a special kind of wriggling called sidewinding. The picture shows a desert rattlesnake called a sidewinder.

The small burrowing owls make their nests in burrows in the ground. They do not dig their own burrows, though. Instead they use holes made by other animals, such as the gopher tortoise.

The young owls, called owlets, come to the entrance of the burrow and wait for their parents to bring them food. If they are disturbed they hiss like angry rattlesnakes to scare **predators** away.

Cactus wrens build their nests in cacti. The nest is a hollow ball of fine plants lined with feathers and hair. This stops the wren and its family from getting too hot by shading them from the sun. When the young wrens have flown away, the parent wrens continue to sleep in the nest. It gets cold in the desert at night and the nest helps to keep the wrens warm.

Index/Glossary